Escape from the Rave Police

By Jon Blake

Illustrated by Colin Mier

Contents

Chapter 1	5
Chapter 2	15
Chapter 3	23
Chapter 4	31
Chapter 5	35
Chapter 6	41
Chapter 7	49

Chapter 1

My name is Eric Wall. I'd like to tell you a complete lie about something that never happened.

It all began on Thursday evening. Mum and Dad were watching Top of the Pops as usual. I'd just got a new game called Death Rabbit 2000, and I wanted the telly.

"In our day, all teenagers watched Top of the Pops," said Dad.

"It ain't your day, is it?" I said.

Mum and Dad ignored me. I sighed out loud, bounced my football, and did my best to annoy them. They still took no notice.

I decided to go for a walk.

Down the road I met Kelly Beck. Kelly looked bored as well.

Want to buy a record?

Not if you've touched it.

Kelly took out the record. It was *Bye Bye Baby* by the Bay City Rollers. I cringed.

"You bought *that*?" I sneered.

"No way!" said Kelly. "I nicked it off Mum."

"What for?"

"She's banned me from the rave."

I grabbed the record. "I'll sling it for you," I said.

"Get off!" said Kelly.

Kelly stuffed the record back in her bag. She would probably put it back in a few days. That was her way.

We walked along aimlessly. There was nowhere to go for people our age. The only place was Queen Street Station. At least it was warm. That's where we went.

We were in for a surprise. Something had happened at the station. There was police tape barring one of the doors. The glass was smashed. But the other door, at the far end, was open.

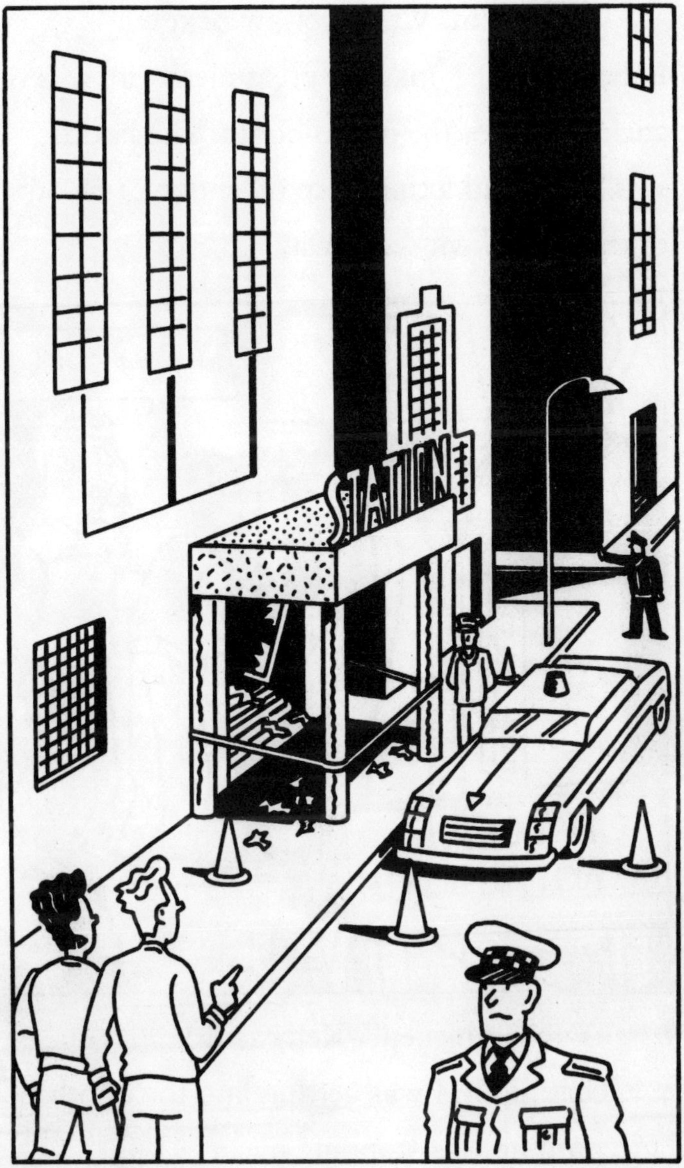
STATION

We went in. What we saw next was unbelievable. A massive great meteorite was sticking out of the photo booth. The booth was black and a thin wisp of smoke came out of the top. I kept well away.

"You're chicken," Kelly said.

That did it. I was getting into the booth and nothing was stopping me.

"Maybe the photo will come out as an alien," I said.

"Same as usual, you mean," said Kelly.

We both climbed into the booth. Everything was cracked and warm to the touch. Kelly took out two pound coins and fed them in.

"You've wasted that!" I said.

I was wrong. Incredibly enough, the little red light came on. There was a hum, then FLASH!

Then I really don't know what happened. It felt like my heart stopped. I didn't know where I was.

"I'm getting out," I said.

I jumped out of the photo booth. The station was completely different. There was a newspaper on the floor, and the date was 10 March, 2079.

13

Chapter 2

There was no doubt about it. We were in the future. There were twice as many office blocks and twice as many beggars. The Capitol Shopping Centre had become Mega Gamesville, and the cinema was showing Terminator 23.

We walked down New Road, which was now called Old Street. It was hard to work out where we were. Then I recognised the Venue. The Venue was the top live music arena. Except it wasn't a live music arena any more. It was a car park.

We walked on. The Ad Lib Club had gone as well. It used to be the best disco in town.

"What's happened to the night-life?" I asked.

"Looks like there isn't any," said Kelly.

We reached my street. That didn't look so different. Same old row of terraces.

Nervously, I rang the doorbell of number twelve.

A long silence, then a young lad's voice: "Who's that?"

"Eric," I replied.

"Eric?" said the voice. "*No one's* called Eric!"

"I've just arrived in a time machine," I explained.

"Oh," said the voice. "You'd better come in."

The door opened. The lad was about my age. He was pale, and his clothes looked like something out of a 1970s Oxfam shop. He told us his name was Charles, but I didn't laugh. Charles was probably a trendy name in 2079.

I explained that I used to live in the house, and wondered what it was like now. Charles showed me in. The whole room was covered in a kind of black felt. The only furniture was a blow-up beanbag sofa and a state-of-the-art smelly-vision.

The smelly-vision, as Charles explained, was a Virtual Reality machine, with touch and smell controls. Charles sat in it to demonstrate. He plugged in a game called

Escape Into Eternity. Soon he had completely forgotten about us. His fingers fiddled madly, and his mouth sucked on a tube called Instant NRG. The tube led down to a bag on his stomach.

"Must be his food supply," said Kelly.

There was also a bag round the back of him, but we had no idea what that was for.

Hours passed. Charles played happily on. I explored the house, but there was nothing to see. I wanted to find out what Charles's records were like, but I didn't discover any. There wasn't even a stereo.

Suddenly there was a loud thump at the door. Kelly and I jumped, but Charles didn't hear a thing.

The thump came again, then a yell: "We know you're in there!"

I shook Charles by the shoulder. He looked round dreamily.

> Charles, I think you'd better –

Too late. There was a massive CRASH and the door was flattened. Four figures burst into the room. They wore riot cop helmets, bulletproof vests, baggy jeans and Air Jordan trainers.

Oh no! The Rave Police!

Chapter 3

One thing was for sure. We were in big trouble. These Rave Police were armed and unhappy.

"Oh dear!" said PC 417. "Oh dear, oh dear, oh dear!"

> I was just going out! Honest, officer, I was on my way!

> In your slippers?

Charles looked guiltily at his feet.

The Rave Police turned to us.

"And what have we here?" asked PC 292.

"More stay-at-homes," said PC 683.

"We'll just have to teach you to enjoy yourselves," said PC 345.

PC 417 took a stun-gun from his holster. "In the van," he barked.

We didn't argue.

We weren't the only teenagers in the police van. A dozen others were already inside. Their hands twitched, their bodies rocked, and their eyes flickered like nervous fleas.

"What's the matter with them?" I asked nervously.

"Some have been on VR machines for weeks," said Charles. "In fact, some still think they are on a VR machine."

"No wonder they're freaking out," said Kelly.

The van moved at incredible speed. We were soon on the outskirts of town.

"Where are they taking us?" I asked.

"Into the country," said Charles.

The van came on to a ten-lane highway called the E6. Three more vans joined us. Soon after that, ten police cars appeared, then a squadron of bikes. Up above, a helicopter circled.

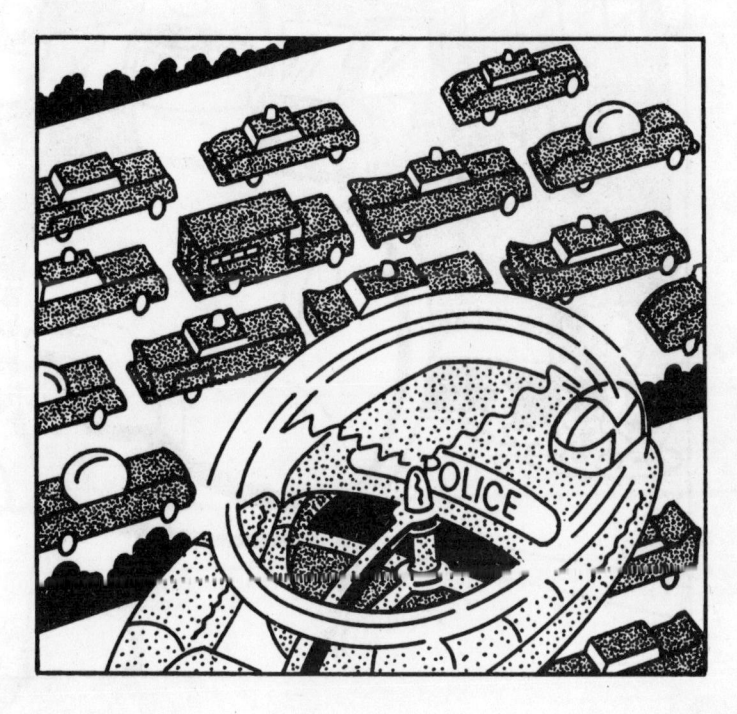

"Is this all for us?" I asked.

"You'll soon see," said Charles.

We moved off the highway and on to a narrow country road. By now the line of police vehicles stretched as far as the eye could see. We drove on a few miles, then came to a deserted airfield. Up ahead was a huge aircraft hangar. The vehicles were stopping in front of it, and a line of teenagers was being frog-marched inside.

We stopped. "Wait there," barked
PC 417. The Rave Police got out of the van.

"What is this place?" asked Kelly.

"What does it look like?" said Charles.

"In our day," I said, "it was the kind of place you'd have a rave."

"That's right," said Charles.

"You mean," said Kelly, "the police have brought us to a rave?"

Charles frowned. "Have you really come out of a time machine?" he asked.

"Honest we have!" I replied.

"In that case," said Charles, "I'd better explain.'

Chapter 4

"Long, long ago," began Charles, "teenagers used to gather in huge numbers to dance. Some of these dances went on all night, or even all weekend. There was very little trouble, because everyone was out for a good time. But for some strange reason, the police kept raiding these dances and arresting everybody. Needless to say, people got fed up with this. They began to give up dancing, and played computer games instead. Dances became few and far between. People stopped buying records. Top of the Pops, a very famous programme, was taken off the air. The government realised it had to do something."

Why?

Because the music industry was going broke. And the music industry is a very important industry.

"So what did they do?" I asked.

"They made dancing compulsory," said Charles.

"Compulsory?" I asked. "What's that?"

"Like school," explained Charles. "It means you have to do it."

"So what happened?" asked Kelly.

"The youth rebelled," said Charles. "They stopped dancing altogether."

What did the government do then?

They got tough. They formed the Rave Police — police officers dedicated to all that is best in music, fashion and movement.

Right on cue, PC 417 opened the van door. "All right, you lot," he said. "Time to get on down."

Chapter 5

At the door of the hangar stood four huge detectives. They were obviously the bouncers. One of them frisked me.

We walked into the building and were hit by a wave of sound and light. The walls were one massive cinema screen, and the music seemed to pulse right out of it. Holograms floated in mid-air.

The mixing desk was like a huge living animal. JUSTICE HEAD SOUND SYSTEM was written on the front of it, and three High Court judges stood behind it.

There was only one problem. No one was dancing. In fact, the scene looked more like a demo. The crowd of teenagers was gathered at one end, refusing to move. The Rave Police were huddled in teams, getting their orders.

I closed my eyes and opened my ears. What incredible music! The beat was primitive, but the sounds were from Mars. They made 90s dance music seem as weak as an old waltz.

"Is it?" said Charles, in a bored voice.

"Don't you think so?" I asked.

"I don't have any musical taste," replied Charles. "None of us has."

Kelly jogged my elbow. Something was happening. One of the Rave Police approached with a megaphone.

"You are blocking the way!" he barked. "Will you please move on to the dancefloor!"

No one moved. Then, suddenly, a youth broke ranks, dashed on to the floor, and started dancing wildly.

> Hey, this is great! Let's dance, everybody.

No one was impressed.

"It's a police agent," explained Charles.

"How do you know?" I asked.

"They're always trying to infiltrate us," said Charles.

I thought this was quite funny. Charles didn't. He looked at me and Kelly with a suspicious eye. "You never know who you can trust," he said.

Chapter 6

The night wore on. The tension grew. It was only a matter of time before the Rave Police made their big move.

It came on the stroke of midnight. The police started forming up in V-shaped squads. The front rows armed themselves with shields and stun-sticks. Suddenly they rushed the crowd.

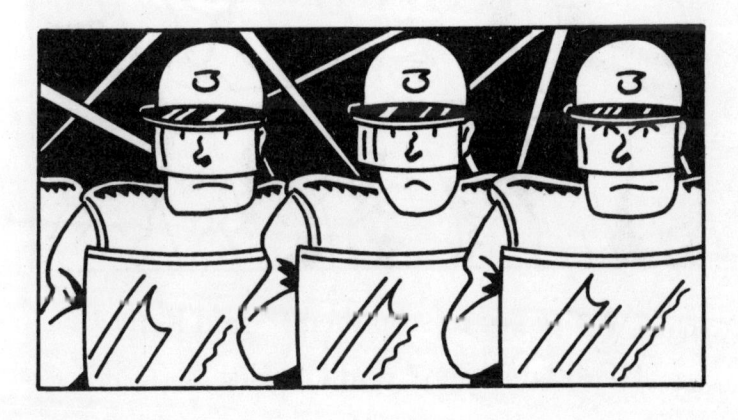

Panic swept through the crowd. Fists flew and stun-sticks thudded. Nine or ten struggling teenagers were pulled on to the dancefloor.

"We've got to stop them!" said Kelly.

"Too late now," said Charles.

It was certainly too late for the nine or ten teenagers. Each of them was surrounded by a gang of cops. To a hidden signal, the Rave Police started grooving, posing, moon-walking and body-popping. The youths were too scared to resist. With stiff, self-conscious movements, they began to dance.

This had a terrible effect on our morale. Next time the snatch squads went in, there was little resistance. The third time, there was no resistance at all.

> It's no use, they're too strong.

"Don't they ever get tired?" I asked.

"No, they never get tired," said Charles. "The music gives them energy."

"How do you know?" I asked.

"Once," said Charles, "the DJ put on the wrong record. It wasn't in the Rave Police Top 40, and it wasn't a rare groove classic. They just seemed to go to pieces."

I pondered on this. All we needed was a really, really dire record. A record so bad it would drain the Rave Police of all energy.

Suddenly, I had an idea. "Kelly," I said. "Have you still got your Mum's single?"

"Yeah. Why?"

"Give it here a sec."

Kelly fished through her bag and brought it out. I sighed with joy as I checked the label – *Bye Bye Baby* by the Bay City Rollers.

"This," I said, "will possibly kill them."

I took the record straight over to the Justice Head Sound System.

"Do you play requests?" I asked.

The judges looked suspicious. "That depends," they said.

"It's a classic," I said, handing them the record.

It was as if I had handed them a diamond. "Vinyl!" they cried. "It's vinyl!"

The judges had all heard of vinyl records, but never actually seen one. They kept an ancient turntable under the decks, just in case. Now, at last, they could put it to use.

> The Rave Police will go wild when they hear this!

I didn't disagree.

The judges fitted the record on to the turntable, and I moved smartly away.

Chapter 7

The effect of *Bye Bye Baby* was electric. The whole dancefloor seemed to grind to a halt. The Rave Police lost all discipline. Some swore at the judges; some argued with each other; and some just slumped to the ground.

I strolled casually through the mayhem. As I saw Charles, I raised one finger on high and did a little victory wiggle.

But Charles was not smiling. In fact, he looked quite angry.

"What's the matter, comrade?" I said.

"You did this!" he snapped.

"Did what?" I asked.

At this point I happened to look behind me. It was then I noticed something alarming.

The dancefloor was filling up.

Before my very eyes, the youth were discovering the joy of music.

My efforts were in vain. Soon almost every teenager was dancing. Only Charles and a few mates stood firm, with their hands around their ears.

"Came in a time machine, eh? You must think we were born yesterday!" said Charles.

Things were looking dangerous. It was time for a sharp exit. We got out of that door without a second to spare.

Luckily the door of the nearest van was open. Luckily Kelly knew how to drive.

Unluckily, so did Charles. We sped off up the country road with Charles and his mates right on our tail. All those computer games had given them excellent reflexes.

It's almost as if they're locked on to us.

Perhaps they are.

We flew down the E6 at half the speed of sound. Charles followed like a heat-seeking missile.

Coming into town we had a whole series of accidents, but nothing which damaged the van. We discovered too late that Queen Street was shut to cars, but somehow we made it to the station.

"Run for it!" said Kelly.

We left the van and dashed for the station door. To our relief, the photo booth was still there. We leapt inside.

"Go!" I screamed.

Nothing happened.

"Have you got two pounds?" asked Kelly.

"No," I replied. "Have you?"

Too late. The footsteps had arrived. "Out of there!" someone barked.

We froze.

"Out of there!" came the voice again.

Suddenly two arms burst through the curtain, grabbed me, and yanked me out.

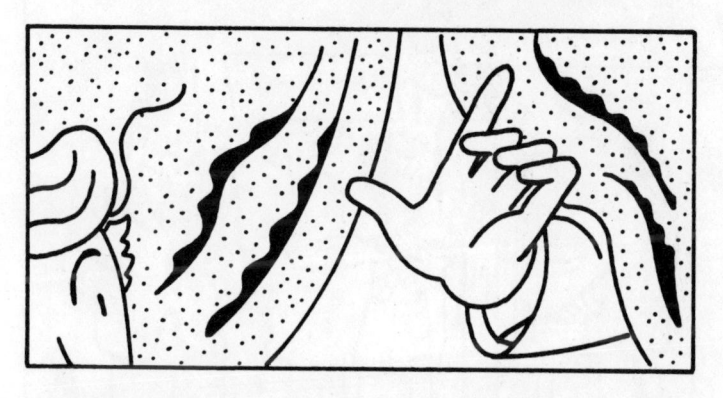

To my amazement, I found myself looking at a police officer, 1990s style.

Next to him was the station manager. The station was completely back to normal.

"Can't you read?" asked the station manager, pointing at the sign which said DANGER.

"I – I've just been to the future," was all I could say.

"No, you haven't, son," said the copper. "You've been under the influence of the mind-bending rays of a Venusian meteorite."

"Oh," I said. "Are you sure?"

"Come on, hop it," said the station manager. "And you," he added, to Kelly. We did as we were told. But I couldn't help glancing back, just to check the copper wasn't wearing trainers.

The funny thing was, Kelly and I had had exactly the same experience. Right down to the last detail.

> So how do we know it didn't happen?

> I know how we can tell.

She reached into her bag. She felt her pockets. Her face dropped. "The record!" she said. "It's gone!"

57

"Then we really did go to the future!" I said.

A terrible thought crossed Kelly's mind. "Maybe we still *are* in the future," she said, "and this is a dream."

We stood, face to face, in fearful confusion. Then Kelly turned on her heel and ran for home. I checked she had turned the corner, then pulled *Bye Bye Baby* out of my jacket and dropped it in the nearest bin.

HUMOUR, SET C

Demons in Diguise *by Jean Ure*

Steven is just about to start his first teaching job. He thinks the boys at the posh school will be well-behaved and polite.

He is in for a nasty surprise!

Colin the Barbarian *by Steve Barlow and Steve Skidmore*

The characters in Colin's computer game have gone on strike!

To his surprise, Colin finds himself in the game for real. Can he make it to the Lord of Pain's castle? And what awaits him if he gets there?

Escape from the Rave Police *by Jon Blake*

It's 2079, and if you don't like to dance, you'd better look out. With the Rave Police about, there's no escape from the party...

ALSO BY JON BLAKE

Crush

TEEN LIFE, SET C

Ian's class have a wild time with their media studies project ... Somehow that video camera seems to land everyone in trouble – especially Ian!

ANOTHER BOOK YOU MIGHT ENJOY ...

I Love Peanut Head

by Pete Johnson

HUMOUR, SET B

Scott's having a really bad week. It doesn't help when Peanut Head, the horrible Headmaster, starts being nice to him. How can he prove he's not Peanut Head's pet?

ANOTHER BOOK YOU MIGHT ENJOY ...

My Secret Love by Andy Brown

by Narinder Dhami

TEEN LIFE, SET D

Andy really likes Beth, but will he ever get to talk to her? Every time they meet, something seems to go wrong!

ANOTHER BOOK YOU MIGHT ENJOY ...

Diary of a Murder

by Terry Deary

HORROR, SET D

Thursday 1 January

A New Year. Time to make New Year's resolutions.

I have just two ...

1   I'm going to use this computer to keep a diary. This diary. This very secret diary.

2   I'm going to kill my grandmother.